content warning:
abuse, death, paranoia, violence, sex.

poems of love

ben st.john

/:

to be yours

crush

everything I need

rainbow's end

spread the love

get you some

swiped

woe is

say my name

loving

meant to be

//:

(if) you left me

the lie

knives

bread

bush

trenches

unwelcome visitor

inside

leading me

bled

what's happened

midsummer's nightmare

stupid me

timeless

wilted roses

never meant to

mine alone

///:

please

stay

falling falling

3rd step

the idea of me

scape

freedom

to you, only for

a day

always, forever

a poem of love

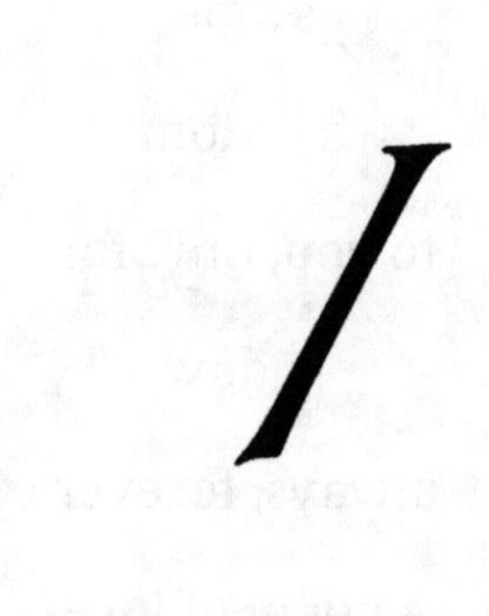

to be yours

something special; more
than another passerby

a dream to have
one everyone knows
to be loved and cherished
just like our parents
and just like them
an eternal bond

like in our stories and tales
a closeness like none other

to be young
in love with someone
those unforgettable butterflies
whenever they're around
their eyes, their smile
how they look at you

how they're around you

if only for

a dream to come true

I'd give this love

like seeds to soil

to take a heart

and make it anew

what I would do for that feeling

what I would do, just for them

I wonder what I am to them
if they'll ever see or think of me
like I do to them?

a glance over to them
idle and still going about their day
sometimes the best moments spent
are moments of brief hiatus
breathing in the space

I wonder if they'll ever know
these feelings I have
it's like heaven came down
and gave one of their angels
a life on earth

what I would give to hold their hand
just for a moment
maybe someone else they're wanting
or if I'm chasing some fantasy
I'm probably bound as another friend

or just another face

to talk to during lunchtime

though, I can't let negativity drag me

nothing is certain but disappointment

if I don't chase this dream

just like the last time

I know good things could happen

I wonder if they know

just what they could mean

if I was given a chance

everything I need, only given more

never alone when not around

life wasn't the same before

and life isn't the same now

it seems like a dream

the way they love me

the world in my hands and

I can't help but just look

at the cracks and curves

bountiful and nature plentiful

the way they adore me

god help me

I'm gonna dive right in

even if sometimes, it isn't perfect

nothing lasts long either way

the worries fade

and the love always returns

rainbow's end

everything needed to want

butterflies

like I've never seen

springtime afternoon

personified perfection

I've never seen the world

through rose-tinted glasses

but the ones in your eyes

there's no need to dream

when you're in front of me

can't imagine my

life before you

can't imagine it now,

without you

everything I've ever wanted

and more.

all the people all the time

all the smiles and the places

I go

always having someone for the day

seldom ever are they alone

making their beachside love

champagne bottles and sunny days

never a worry in their world

despite the world falling right behind

everybody on this earth looking

how happy

smiling and purely oblivious

you need a body

somebody – anybody

cause everybody's gotta get some

and nobody wants to be stagged

who would ever want to spend

their life, a hand on the mouse

and the other reaching for lotion?

from me to you

I hope somewhere inside you know

you're never gonna get it

less you get it together

less you get with the times

be yourself,

but not too much now

a million faces to choose from

swipe of a finger; push of a button

before your eyes a bouquet is thrown

the pretty face behind door #2

hailing from the city

she likes the things you do

and more as you'll find out

you don't wanna miss out

you could find the one

live happily ever after

like your favorite stories

never good enough to have

never have enough to give

maybe this being alone

is all I'll ever be

dying alone is my fate

just like those before me

too good to be true

they always chase for hurt

and curse at their feet

when they finally give way

and fall like debris

maybe I'm deserving

thinking I'm deserving of

something more than myself

when myself cannot give to others

what I can't give to myself

what I never had at all

you're better than they are

but is that much to have?

whatever shall come for us

and whatever is given to us

it's better than this feeling of

never having anything to have

like bankruptcy for the homeless

even if I shouldn't

somehow I know I should

my tank won't fill itself

oh, baby

you know how to treat

me right

how I want, how I need

you bring it to the table

with legs wide open

lying on

your back

call out my name

like I'm your savior

lips like velvet

in your skin

on my mind like suicide

those curves could kill someone

at your altar

on knees and praying for

that special love

always, ever for you.

loving me is exhausting

loving you is punishment

if life is but a dream

I hope to awake soon enough

nightmares I've had

now appear as lucid trips

when compared to you

"my one and only" a great fib

only anyone but you is the one for me

not to get ahead of myself

and let these frustrations blind

hurting ourself will not progress

what's left into anything new

we know this

we can make it work

we were meant to be

this only takes time

just because we're apart doesn't

mean we can't be together

it's just obstacles

so much that's been done

to get to where we were

stick here with me

and never leave my side

we were meant to be

don't feel sorry

no mistakes or regrets

what's done has been done

forever cannot wait anymore for us

we were meant to be

//

(If) You
Left Me

you know I can't leave you

nothing's right in the world

if one day you left

I just wanna wait and see

what you've got to offer

you know you've got it

maybe not for you but definitely me

you know my heart's so giving

for someone like you

for someone like myself

we gave each other our trust

past whatever happens

we would always

consult when we had to

every needed word was spoken

I caught you in our bed

that wench who you preferred

I gave you my body

but they had the better edges

sharp turns I never had

I let you back in

the fool I was

to think you would change

old habits die hard

I wish you did too

despite us,

all of this love is suffering

I'd rather feel these knives

tearing me away

than have you leave

never

out of my head

other's touch a blasphemous action

not a mark, not a hair

I want inside your cage

throw away the key

I'll stay inside forever

Bush

opened gated

garden always visited

lost the flavor

same as it was

other's givings

sweeter than theirs

lord, help me

temptation abides

unfamiliar field

unsure if unsafe

but damned if I am

a home away from

tells me to

pick their fruit

savor every flavor

a sweetness sickening

I tell them

take it away from

me at once

Trenches

to be yours

used to hiding away

these tunnels and hideaways

I dug long ago

every day your hand

never I trusted to hold

never I trusted to help

I had to grab it

take these jabs

trust you'd be there

I found out

that's what it's like

being in love

I let you inside

you said I'd survive

be right there beside

stupid of me

you kept lying to me

laughed when I wanted to cry

in the morning in you

thinking about

the nasty things about you

body's grip like chokehold

hypnotize like gold

you know how to make me beg

for more, or when you're at the door

know you'll be gone soon

pack my bags

as I pack yours

guess I never knew

how to keep you sane

how to keep you in-tact

suns up and spirits down

nothing could keep us here

blank faces staring in bed

like looking at headstones

you take me out

but won't take me in

not so soon

life is passing by

my final breath

will be meeting here soon

lead me back home

not to some taxi

don't drive me far away

Bled

every time I bled

the same old cause,

my own two hands

forcing you as my cover

for my own mistakes

cursing and hating you

through every second of your help

I turned with a covered ear

bring back yesterday

never let me let go

never once was

never mine

where are you hiding?

if you could find me,

would you keep it again?

is it lost or,

never meant to be found?

afraid to let go of

you

but even more terrified of

you leaving first

*Midsummer's
Nightmare*

do you still see me as I

have seen you before?

do you still even see me at all?

had we never met

that name never touched

my lips

I would be the same

type of miserable

as I am with you

you're a different shade of

black

hands visible

but I can't find my way

in the endless darkness

I couldn't lose you

even if you killed me

I'd be stuck

I don't wanna hurt you

but I know time has come

I could bring the moon

you'd complain about the craters

I hope I never know

whoever's next

how'd they feel around you

I haven't let go

as my hands were bleeding

you told me over and over

to cover my bruises

I wanted to show you

I could've been good to you

never a thought to be

anything less than what

could help you, in the end

the more I tried

the more you got tired

every fight we would have

always my fault somehow

you were always there

I tried to be more

when I should've left as is

I accepted we could only go

through the same fights

over and over before fatigue

I don't blame you

for wanting to sleep it off

where have you been?

is there time for us?

more

life has us going elsewhere

mine without your direction.

Wilted

Roses

try my best, all I can do

but there is just no pleasing you

even if I were to

turn water into wine

you would still want the water

the best moments we had

came and left as we learnt each other

your ways like an outdated atlas

going everywhere that shouldn't be

I had to guide you correctly

nothing ever to your eye

has that quality you want

deserving of the best

yet still choosing me

as if I'm a servant

never meant to

harm or to scar

nothing I can control

you will heal

just stay calm

it was only accidental

you always overreact

always make a fuss

to minor things

always twisting words

making me look bad

never said that

it's no wonder

you're stuck with me

you keep choosing wrong

ending up with people

just like me

you'll be just alone

like abandoned pets in rain

begging for return

Mine
Alone

in mine alone

who are you without me?

a lost runt

unloved and unwanted

nothing without my help

nothing without my love

no one loves you like me

pleasures or spoils you like me

even if someone else did

they wouldn't do it like me

I'm the only one

poor whore, all alone again

hurting myself plenty

all the blame to give

for this hell I live

I told you what I needed

so why act surprised?

you used to run back to me

like you had nowhere else to go

so why not come back?

no restraining order

can keep me from you

everything I did for you

so ungrateful and needy

I don't need you

like you don't need me

run to your new parasite

they'll treat you better than I did

this hell I feel

this is all your fault

Please   come back to

me

a glass is not full until

you're there to fill

it up again

thirsty and desiccated

without yours

what will I do without

you?

spend my life finding

replicas or wax figures?

some body to figure

like yours once did

what happened to

us?

nothing that I did could've

brought it to this

nothing said, done, or delivered

unsent texts

would've kept it straight

return to me

only you to calm
to sleep, dream, live
fuck whatever I had said.

what will it take for you to love me?

fix myself up in clean clothes and cologne

get a nice job with a new car and house

a dog and a big, soft bed

everything you wanted as long as you will.

what will it take for you to enjoy me?

take you out on expensive dates

stare at the moon and the distant stars

kiss you and show adoration

just for you to leave me

everything you wanted as long as you will

what will it take for me to prove myself?

meaningless apologies for the things I never did

cheap plastic gifts at the corner drug store

meet your parents and give a good first impression

everything you wanted as long as you will

what will it take for you to stay?

begging on my knees

crying like a buffoon

leave me alone and you'll leave me to die

everything you wanted as long as you will

as long as you stay

I will make all your days

worthwhile and beautiful with a smile on your face

you gave me something that I never had

dreams in my mind that I could complete

happy for the first time in ages

so as long as you stay

to whichever god I pray

that maybe just today

everything could be normal

just like before

as long as you stay

everything will be normal

normal, again.

Falling
Falling

never meant

built to die

born to fall like

leaves in the summer

we never found

loneliness remains

when you're beside me

as if you never met.

it's never really over with you

sometimes outside the window

a face I see looks just like you

thinking I'm being followed

thinking my home isn't alone

goddamn you, just leave me

only when together did

you did so

be you locked up or in a casket

countries away or in the next city

I still feel you beside me

and I want your memories

to die off finally

not even disease

would stay with me this long

I'd kill you if I could

but I don't want to hurt you more

that's what you would've wanted

everything you did to me

it's all just your effort

to make me debilitated

goodbye hasn't done so much

as you have done to me

all I could or can do

is go on

and live

something you never let me do.

one of many

soon to be nothing

passing stare

I said I missed them

they said "just the idea"

if that's what they call it,

I wonder what

you'd call these tears

a void of presence

that ringing noise

where your voice once filled

they've moved on

and I have too

but it still terrifies me

the simple idea of

what was.

Scape

it was too soon to know

too young to tell

too much to handle

not enough to keep

the best things

always happen in prematurity

then they die

long after it gets old

I found myself

swearing at the mirror

things I could avoid

hooked up on

empty nothings

just so I could

feel better about

everything I never faced.

It's over

but not for me

try as I must

hard as I work

there's no

way from out of you

the things you did

no man ever should

no one should suffer

but I had to

...why?

what did I do

to merit this abuse?

what did I say

or never spoke?

I just wanted

the best for you, but

you never thought of

what I could use

punches you pulled

covers to wear

the worst of it

I'd fix you if

I didn't have to fix myself

only you've made me

worry about tomorrow

worrying wake

tomorrow you'll return

for now, I just

want some peace

away from you.

I don't believe in soulmates

it's a matter of time and chance

love and chaos go hand in hand

decades given in a span of seconds

nor do I believe

in love at first sight

sometimes what's needed

is waiting in the dark

I put my faith

into my future with you

even if tomorrow doesn't come

you'll be there

to spend whatever

A Day

a day to have

to spend with you

a day of grief

of losing you

no matter, my darling

past it all

a reunion is bestowed

one day, again.

clouds of sorrow beckon tears and longing

an empty space in the sheets, irreplaceable

standing next to her inert and barren body

decades and decades, too soon to leave

through joy, memories, children

ice cream in summer, jackets in the fall

slow dancing in the kitchen, champagne on new years

birthdays and candles, rollercoasters and bumper cars

grocery aisles and prepping dinner

and though I know, the sour moments

the arguments and yelling

illness of body and mind

I made a promise

till the moment I held her hand goodbye

I would be there

on her hospital bed, that last kiss

she told me how much she loved me

I knew it true, she never let go

though I said goodbye

I never left her alone

my heart's still full

with the love and promise she gave

through my tears, you still smile

I feel your love from worlds away

my love, always and forever

I hope to see you again

another kiss, I'll see you tomorrow

goodnight, my love.

if you should keep

and never forget

all I ask

don't leave

one and only

until none forever

I lay naked in front of you

no worries

nothing to lose

if I lose you

nothing to keep

my promises

black days inevitable

until they're gone

it's only today

there's nothing I can do
but give you everything

no guarantee
futures can end
between now and about to
sharing gravity,
pulse, and entropy

though I cannot
tell you how it ends
I can tell
there's only
what we have

a moment

nothing more.

bonus poems

and still, I felt that crisp breeze of early spring's breath

that dark night, last I saw your face

that last kiss before you drove home

few hours were like few countries away

I missed you, I did

I missed you

flowing waves of golden silk, as your head

lay softly on my chest

hearing your breath, feeling your heart

the ambiance of perfect seconds had

looped in my head like a broken record

yet, it was a song that lulled me

and after that night, we lasted no more

I spat my blasphemies at you

without second thought or reason

you left me soon after

without needing second thought or reason

tried as I did for your return

seasons and months passed

but not the thought of you

felt the phantom of your touch

haunting my thoughts never-ending

what was it about you

that made me ache and yearn?

never knew I could feel this way

for someone who never stayed

you found better, I'm still looking

harsh as it was, it was truth

maybe it was because you loved me

that made me want more

than I ever would have

that feeling I never grasped

before it fell from my hands

now I have to go on

just like you already have

hoping chance can bring someone

like you, again

and still, wondering what could've been

more time in my arms with you

I hope you're doing well, now

I hope whoever comes next

holds on tighter than I ever did.

T-Shirt

when you thought of my t-shirt

you wore it each night

like an endless hug

like I'm still there

like I never left

like goodbye was never said.

sleepless weeping echoes wailing

swimming alone guided by moonlight

guide me through the dark

alone in the night without your hush

I gave; but it wasn't enough

I spoke every wrong word

I promised but I didn't keep

you told me what you needed

I didn't listen close enough

don't worry about me now,

that's my job to do

overdue for maintenance

just another worn machine

I'll be out running soon as you know

being young is a hidden tragedy

enough time to grow

but to grow is to know

that I won't know enough to see

hard truths that'll come to me later

you're one I'll remember

it's on my mind now

a step forwards can be backwards

when your eyes are closed

and you don't know where to go

my youth is a curse

time to see more

but unknowing of tomorrow

sorrow that will come

of losing you

too young to keep

too young to know

too young to understand

what it means to be adult

I said my curses

I couldn't take back

my first love...

...first...

how many steps does it take

before the correct decision is made?

how many X's in your oh's

before you finally know?

your generation and mine

show the differences in our choice

take our time

to find the right one

to avoid any unneeded struggle

who wants a 3rd wife?

why not get it right

the first time?

who'd want to fail their kids?

who'd want to make them think

mom and dad hate each other?

no greater nightmare

than repeating the past

and never learning from it.

Free

Men

free men are often the loneliest

no friends or partners

to talk over coffee

just familiar faces in supermarkets

to see and hide away from.

Never

an

Only

always will there be someone else

stronger, sexier, happier, loving

maybe not their first choice, per se

but mostly just a choice

maybe the only one

the myth of open relationships

you were always just another choice

if they can't find someone else,

well then, they're stuck with you

and you're stuck too

with someone who feels stuck with you

if it's not worth another day

don't give anymore

mistakes are inevitable

but from each new error

old mistakes are kept away

but if they could choose

and they still choose you

never you worry

cause they know that you're

all they could ever want.